A Family In Australia

LIBRARY OF CONGRESS CATALOGING-IN-PUBLICATION DATA

Browne, Rollo.
   A family in Australia.

   Previously published as: Australian mining family.
   Summary: Describes the home, school, amusements, customs, and work
of a twelve-year-old boy and his family living in a remote town in the
Northern Territory of Australia.
   1. Northern Territory—Social life and customs—Juvenile literature.
2. Aluminum mines and mining—Australia—Northern Territory—
Juvenile literature. 3. Family—Australia—Northern Territory—Juvenile
literature. [1. Australia—Social life and customs. 2. Family life—
Australia] I. Fairclough, Chris, ill. II. Title
DU395.B76   1987   994.29′5   86-20103
ISBN 0-8225-1671-3 (lib. bdg.)

Manufactured in the United States of America

   2   3   4   5   6   7   8   9   10   97   96   95   94   93   92   91   90   89

A Family In Australia

Rollo Browne

Photographs by Chris Fairclough

Lerner Publications Company • Minneapolis

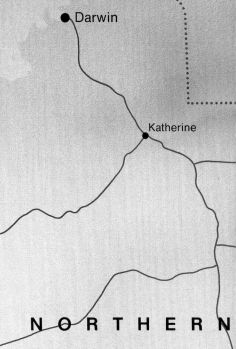

A R A F U R A

Darwin

Katherine

N O R T H E R N

David Baker lives in Nhulunbuy in the Northern Territory of Australia. He is 12 years old and has three older brothers. Stephen is 14, Robert is 17, and Kevin is 19—he's left home already.

David and his brothers live with their parents in a house in the oldest part of Nhulunbuy. Even that's not very old, because the town was built just before the Bakers moved there. They moved to Nhulunbuy right after David was born, so they've lived there as long as he can remember.

Nhulunbuy is a mining town built on the tip of the Gove Peninsula. It's about 385 miles (620 kilometers) by airplane from Darwin, the capital of the Northern Territory.

S E A

Nhulunbuy
Gove • Cape Arnhem
Peninsula • Yirrkala

A R N H E M
L A N D *Blue*
Mud *Gulf*
ABORIGINAL *Bay*
RESERVE

of

Carpentaria

• Borroloola

T E R R I T O R Y

QUEENSLAND

N

↑

0

0   300 km

150 mi

To get to Nhulunbuy, you can fly from Darwin in the west or from Cairns in northern Queensland in the east. Planes land at Nhulunbuy about five times a week, but jumbo jets don't land there because the runway is too short.

There are no roads from Nhulunbuy to the rest of the Northern Territory, except a rough track that goes through Arnhem Land and comes out near Katherine.

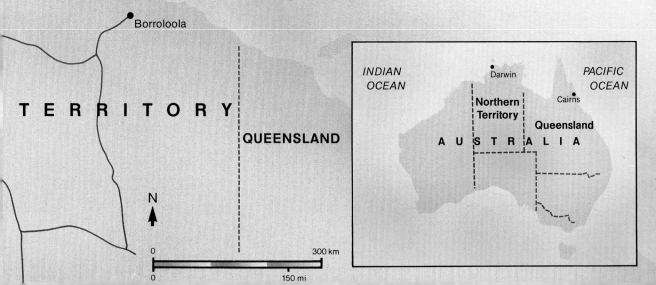

INDIAN
OCEAN • Darwin *PACIFIC*
OCEAN

Northern
Territory • Cairns

Queensland

A U S T R A L I A

The road to Katherine is only passable in the dry season, between April and October. Even then, most people use a four-wheel-drive truck, and it takes two or three days to get through.

The rest of the year the river crossings can be flooded by the rains. David's family never travels out of Nhulunbuy by road. They always take the plane.

If they just want to go out into the country around Nhulunbuy, they have to have a permit. All the land around Nhulunbuy is part of the Arnhem Land Aboriginal Reserve and belongs to the Aboriginal people. Anyone who isn't Aboriginal needs a permit to go outside the town or mine boundaries.

There are about 4,000 people living in Nhulunbuy and most of them work for the mine. David's father, Tom, works there as a powder monkey. The term "powder monkey" comes from the boys who carried gunpowder to the guns on sailing ships. Mr. Baker uses high explosives to break up the bauxite. Bauxite is the rock that is mined at Nhulunbuy and it's used to make aluminum. The mine at Gove is one of the biggest and richest bauxite mines in Australia.

David has watched his dad blasting a couple of times, but he watched from a long way away because of the danger of falling rocks. The explosion is always exciting to see.

Rows of holes are drilled in the ground, and then Mr. Baker wires the holes to the main fuse which will set off the explosion. When the holes are all wired, he fills them up with explosive from the truck. Then the truck blocks the road so that no one can drive into the blasting area. The mine is close to the airport, so Mr. Baker calls to get the "all-clear." If there are any planes around, he has to wait until they are safely out of the way.

Then his driver starts the get-away car and keeps the engine running while Mr. Baker lights the fuse. They have exactly three minutes to get clear before the explosion.

David's mother worries about Mr. Baker getting hurt, but he's always very careful. The real danger comes when some of the explosives don't go off. Then he has to go back to find out what went wrong. He says that the blasting is easy because the bauxite is so close to the surface. It is much easier to work in open-pit mines like Gove than in underground mines.

When the blasting is finished, the loaders begin filling the dump trucks with loose bauxite. The dump trucks are huge and can carry over 78 tons (80 metric tons). Sometimes visitors climb into the cabin for a ride to the crusher.

In the crusher, the bauxite is broken into smaller pieces. Then it travels for ten and a half miles (17 kilometers) on a conveyor belt to the processing plant. The conveyor is covered so the bauxite doesn't get wet when it rains. It's one of the longest conveyor belts in the world.

The processing plant is a huge factory where they start turning the bauxite into aluminum. The plant is right next to the wharf where the ships load up. David's dad says the bauxite is carried all over the world, to Iceland, Egypt, Japan, Switzerland, and the U.S.A.

Mr. Baker knows a lot about rocks from working with them all the time. He collects different kinds of rocks and minerals and David likes to help. Once Mr. Baker found a piece of meteorite which had fallen to earth from space. He sent it to Queensland to be tested to find out what minerals were in it.

A small part of the Arnhem Land Aboriginal Reserve at Gove is rented to the mining company. Everybody in David's family is on the same permit so they can go out into "the bush"—that's what they call the countryside.

Most of the Aboriginal people in the area live in their own community in Yirrkala about 10 miles (16 kilometers) away. People from Nhulunbuy can go to Yirrkala without a permit to buy paintings and things from the Aboriginal craft shop. David is trying to talk his mother into letting him buy a boomerang at the shop.

Cape Arnhem has lots of sandy beaches, but it takes a four-wheel-drive vehicle to get through the sand. David likes standing up in the back of the truck as they travel. The road to the Cape is narrow and bumpy and they have to be careful not to be hit by branches. Some of the branches have green ants' nests in the leaves, and the nests could dump ants all over anyone who hit them.

They have to take fresh water with them when they go to Cape Arnhem, because there are only a few small creeks or springs. But there are lots of good places to camp by the beach or among the sand dunes.

The wind is always blowing and has carved strange shapes in the cliffs and rocks. They can also see a lot of wildlife there, like sea eagles and bush turkeys. The Aborigines hunt and eat the turkeys as well as ducks, emus, big lizards called *goannas*, and occasionally buffalo. No one else is allowed to shoot any wildlife on Aboriginal land. If the Bakers want to go shooting, they use the rifle range at Nhulunbuy.

The buffalo aren't like the ones in the United States. The buffalo in Australia come from tame buffalo that were brought over from Asia. Some got loose and now there are wild buffalo in many parts of the country. They aren't afraid of people and sometimes even come into town looking for food in the gardens. They get mad if they're teased, so everyone just leaves them alone.

15

David and his friends spend a lot of time at the Surf Lifesaving Club on Town Beach. The Club has all kinds of boats, canoes, and boards, and it teaches how to use them and how to rescue people from drowning.

The Surf Club has a crocodile watch tower, but crocodiles don't come into the shallow water at Town Beach very often. They stay in the creek mouths and in the harbor where they can find food.

A man was taken by a crocodile about four and a half miles (6 kilometers) away. He was diving at a reef near the mouth of a saltwater creek. When he didn't come back, a search party went looking for him. They found his body stuck under a log. The crocodile was keeping him to eat later. One of the Aboriginal rangers shot the crocodile near its nest.

There are signs everywhere on the beach warning swimmers about the box jellyfish. These jellyfish are in the ocean in the wet season, usually from November to March, but the signs warn people about swimming between October and May. The Australians call them sea wasps because they have a deadly sting. The shock of a sea wasp sting can kill a person, especially anyone with a weak heart.

The Surf Club keeps vinegar to treat the stings, and David and his friends know what to do. He admits that they worry about the jellyfish—but it doesn't stop them from surfing.

GOVE PENINSULA S.L.S.C.

DANGER

STINGERS

IT IS DANGEROUS TO SWIM IN THESE
WATERS BETWEEN OCTOBER & MAY

Every Sunday during the dry season, when there aren't any sea wasps in the water, the Surf Club holds races for children. Usually, there are events like swimming, board paddling, and rescue. David's brother Robert wins most of the races. David and his two brothers and his best friend Mark are in the junior boat crew. They train in the new boat, the *Crocodile I*.

No one swims near the wharf because there are too many sharks and crocodiles. The water is very deep and full of fish near the wharf. Sometimes David's family fishes there, and they even go into the shallow water to net some small fish for bait.

To catch fish for bait, David's dad wades in about waist deep with his dragnet. He holds the bottom of the net down on the sea bed with his foot, and the top of the net in his hand. David or one of his brothers holds the other end of the net in the shallow water and they sweep it slowly along, then up onto the beach.

The Bakers catch small fish like garfish or hardyhead for bait. The bait is best while it's still alive, so they put the fish into a bucket of water until they want to use one. They put sinkers on their fishing lines to make the bait swim near the bottom, then they put out their lines and wait. David says it's a shock when the big fish strike, because they hit so hard.

The last time the Bakers went fishing, they caught two trevally. The Bakers eat a lot of fish. David says it doesn't matter how his mom cooks it, the fish always tastes good—especially with his favorite vegetable, potatoes with thick onion sauce.

Mrs. Baker works at home. She does the housework, cooking, and shopping, but everyone else does their share, too.

David's mom says she doesn't miss the big city because it's so crowded there. One thing she does miss is being able to get fresh food from the store. Most of the food in the supermarket is frozen, and Mrs. Baker says fresh food is too expensive. Everyone in Nhulunbuy drinks powdered milk, too, because they can't get it fresh.

After a vacation, Mrs. Baker always brings back meat, fresh vegetables, milk, bread, and house plants—things that they can't buy in Nhulunbuy.

David's mom and dad both put a lot of work into their yard. When they first moved in, the ground was bare because the mining company had cleared it for building. Now they have some of the tallest trees in town.

David's family has two pets. Their budgie or parrot is named Pretty Boy, and he can talk a little. He can say "shut up" and "give us a beer." At night they let him out of his cage and he flies around the room. Whiskey, the big blue Persian cat, stays inside all day and doesn't even chase the bird.

Feeding the pets is David's job. He and his brothers have different jobs around the house, like washing dishes, cleaning their rooms, and taking out the garbage. They don't get an allowance, so they have jobs to earn money. David baby-sits, Rob works most weekends as a dishwasher at the hotel, and Stephen does some work for one of their teachers who is building a house.

All the houses built in Nhulunbuy have to be very strong to stand up to the cyclones. The winds get very strong and the sea can flood the town. Cyclones are also called hurricanes in the West Indies and typhoons in the North Pacific. They only hit Australia during the wet season, when it is very hot and steamy and rains a lot.

Mr. Baker is cyclone warden of their street. His job is to make sure that everyone knows when a cyclone is coming, and to tell them to put away anything that's lying around in their yards. The wind can pick up anything loose and turn it into a dangerous weapon.

No cyclone has hit Nhulunbuy yet. The town was put on red alert for Cyclone Cathy but it missed them, and went on to wipe out the town of Borroloola.

Nhulunbuy has two television stations. One is relayed
through satellite dishes just outside town. The other station
sends out programs that are copied from a television station
in Darwin. It takes time to get the programs sent from
Darwin, so David and his family watch news and programs
that are already two days old.

David likes watching sports, and he plays a lot, too. His favorite sport is Rugby league. It's sort of a combination of football and soccer. David's friend Mark and he are on the Walkabout team in the under-13 league. David's been playing every Saturday for three years, but he still gets nervous before the game. He feels all right once they start—especially once he can get the ball and run. He thinks they can win this year.

The St. John's Ambulance Brigade always comes to Saturday games in case anyone gets hurt. David's brother Robert is a member and takes his turn to be on duty. Rob's main hobby is a huge shell collection which he has kept for years. He has more than a thousand shells.

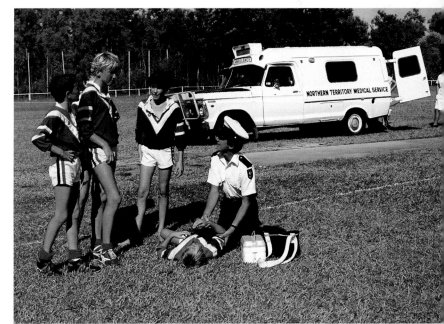

David goes to school in Nhulunbuy. His favorite subjects are sports, mathematics, and computing. Some children leave Nhulunbuy and go to school down south, but David never wanted to leave home and go to a boarding school.

David and his family are ready to go away from Nhulunbuy on vacation. They usually go to Cairns in Queensland. David really likes it there because there's so much to do. After Cairns, he thinks Nhulunbuy is the best place to be. He doesn't think he's missing out even though he lives such a long way from anywhere.

David doesn't want to work at the mine when he leaves school. He really wants to be a policeman, especially one who works with dogs. But he knows he'll have to leave Nhulunbuy to do that.

The Founding of Australia

Australia's first settlers, the Aborigines, arrived there about 40,000 to 50,000 years ago. The first known European to land on Australia was Willem Jansz, a Dutchman. He stopped there in 1606. In 1770, James Cook of the British navy became the first to land on Australia's east coast. Cook claimed the area for Great Britain and named it New South Wales.

Before the Revolutionary War in the United States, Britain had shipped convicts to its American colonies to ease crowding in its jails. Convicts are people put in jail because of crimes they have committed. After the United States won its independence, Britain had to send its convicts somewhere else. In 1787, the first load of male and female convicts started for New South Wales, along with marine guards and their families. They founded the first white settlement in Australia.

The new colony supported itself by farming. Soon the government began to grant land to military officers and freed convicts. Free settlers began to come from England. The settlers began to explore the continent, and some moved to another part of Australia and founded the colony of Victoria.

In 1851, gold was found in New South Wales. A few months later, an even richer gold field was discovered in Victoria. Another field was found in Western Australia, so rich the gold could be broken off the rocks in lumps. Thousands of prospectors from overseas rushed to the gold fields. Many decided to stay in Australia, and the population soared.

Britain stopped shipping convicts to the colonies of Australia by 1868. More than 160,000 convicts had been shipped to Australia since 1788. The Australian colonies were granted independence from Britain by the 1890s, and were united into one country on January 1, 1901.

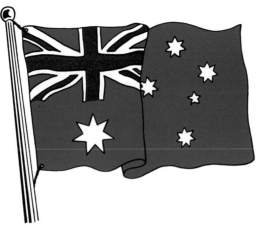

Facts about Australia

Official Name: Commonwealth of Australia

Capital: Canberra

Language: English

Money: Australian dollar

Area: 2,966,150 square miles (7,682,300 square kilometers) including Tasmania
Australia is the only country that is also a continent. It is the smallest continent but the sixth largest country. It is about five-sixths the size of the United States.

Population: About 16 million people
Most people live along the coast, especially in the southeast, where there is enough rainfall. The rest of the country is mostly desert or dry grassland. Australia has about as many people as New York state.

NORTH
AMERICA

SOUTH
AMERICA

EUROPE

ASIA

AFRICA

AUSTRALIA

31

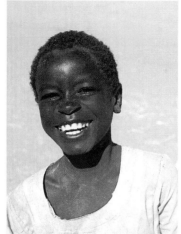

Families the World Over

Some children in foreign countries live like you do. Others live very differently. In these books, you can meet children from all over the world. You'll learn about their games and schools, their families and friends, and what it's like to grow up in a faraway land.

Lerner Publications Company, 241 First Avenue North, Minneapolis, Minnesota 55401

DATE DUE

MAR. 1 8 1991			
MAY 0 8 1992			
NOV. 1 9 1992			
OCT. 1 2 1993			
JAN. 0 7 1998			
APR 1 3 2000			